Seek & Find in the Land of Dinosaurs
First Edition
© [2024] by Jamie Whimsy. All rights reserved.

ISBN: 9798884578319
Published by KaleidoKids Publishing
Printed in United States of America

This book is a work of fiction. Names, characters, places, and incidents either are products of the author's imagination or are used fictitiously. Any resemblance to actual persons, living or dead, events, or locales is entirely coincidental.

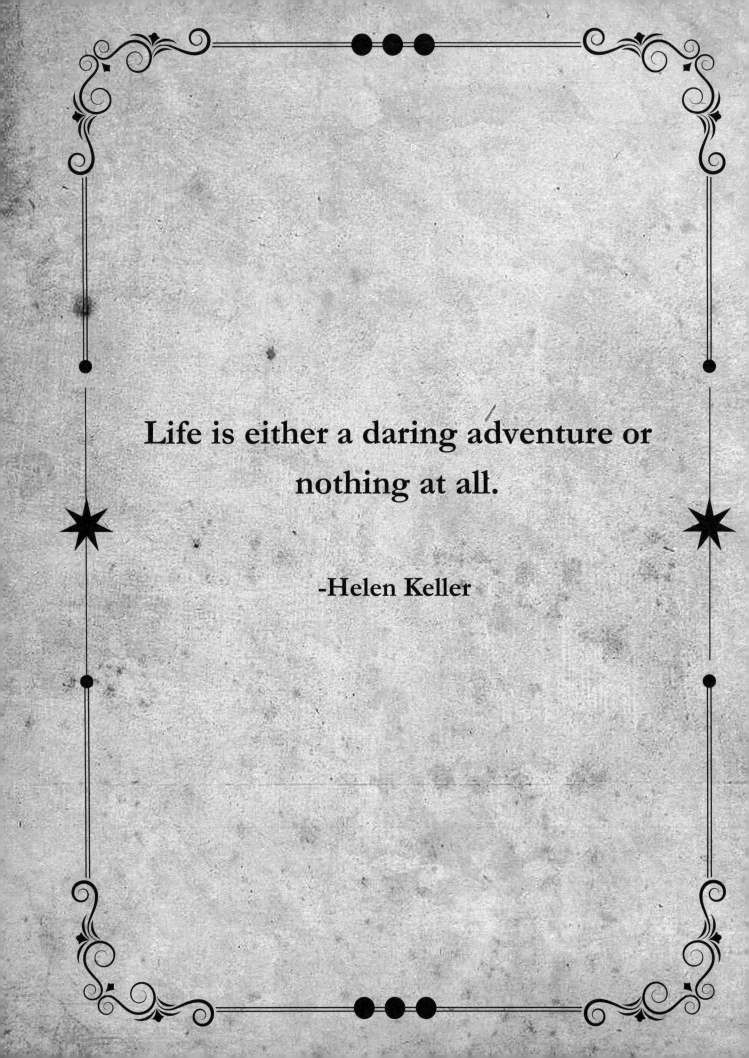

Life is either a daring adventure or nothing at all.

-Helen Keller

TABLE OF CONTENTS

p5-7

It all starts in the attic....

To Prehistoric day

p8-9

Triassic Jungle
(250m years back)

p10-11

Triassic Desert
(230m years back)

p12-13

Triassic Riverbank
(200m years back)

p14-15

Jurassic Coastal Plains
(165m years back)

p16-17

Jurassic Jungle
(160m years back)

p18-19

Jurassic Volcanic Landscape
(150m years back)

p20-21

Cretaceous Floodplains
(120m years back)

p22-23

Cretaceous Forest
(100m years back)

p24-25

Cretaceous Swamps
(80m years back)

p26-27

Cretaceous Coastal Cliffs
(75m years back)

p28-29

Cretaceous Plains Migration
(70m years back)

p30-31

K-Pg Boundary
(66m years back)

Back to present day

p32-33

Dino Mysteries Revealed

Welcome to an Adventure Through Time!

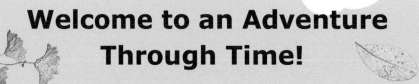

Hello, Time Travelers!
Get ready for an exciting journey from the dawn of the dinosaurs to their mysterious end. This book is your portal to ancient worlds, filled with hidden treasures and fascinating facts.

-Solo Explorers: Keep an eye out for secret items on each page. Please note sometimes they may look smaller or tilted than from Professor Dino's clues.

-Team Quests: Challenge your friends to a seek-and-find race. Who will uncover the hidden wonders first?

-Family Journeys: Share this adventure with your loved ones. Read together, discover, and learn about the majestic dinosaurs and their eras.

Each page is a new adventure, blending fun with learning. Dive in at your own pace, and let curiosity be your guide.

Happy Discoveries!

Jamie Whimsy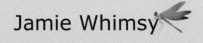

Max, a super cool dinosaur fan, sets off a treasure hunt in the attic of his old house. He finds a lot of old stuff and interesting storybooks about adventures. Suddenly, Max spots a big, odd-looking egg covered in dust.

To his surprise, the egg begins to shimmer and grows bigger and bigger as it hovers mid-air.

What is this? Max wonders and touches it.

Woosh! The egg turns into a kind-looking professor! And he stands in front of the astonished Max with a big smile!

Wow! That's amazing!

Hello Max! I'm Professor Dino, I help kids unlock secrets about dinosaurs. Thanks for waking me up!

As it turns out, Professor Dino can help with time travel too! With a mysterious grin on his face, he nudges Max to open the attic door.

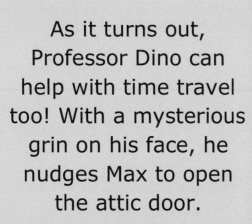

Max is so intrigued as he opens the door, and he is greeted by breathtaking views of the dinosaur age!

Well, that's a hard one, as I still miss a few items from the dinosaur age to complete the puzzle. Can you help me travel back in time to retrieve them? Only by then the secrets can be revealed.

Professor! How did dinosaurs vanish?

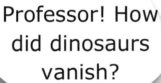

As a young explorer, Max is so thrilled about the quest! Professor Dino hands him a map with all the items to be collected, saying 'My courageous Max, now go past the door as the pre-historic adventure awaits you, and I wish you the best of luck!'

Max pops out of the time machine door into a huge, misty **Triassic Jungle** some 250 million years back! Enormous ferns are everywhere and cycad trees reach sky-high. It's so quiet except for insect buzzes and some distant sounds. 'This place is so cool!' Max says to himself and he just can't wait to find all the hidden objects from Professor Dino's map!

The Her-re-ra-saurus, big and impressive, walks through the forest like a warrior. This strong hunter marks the early days when dinosaurs begin to rule the land. Imagine a dinosaur race: the Herrerasaurus could have been the all-time gold medalist, winning each race like a breeze.

If you think you're fast, you haven't seen me at lunchtime! #SpeedySnacker

The Eo-raptor, one of the earliest dinosaurs, dashes through the bushes. Tiny and super fast, this little creature is the starting chapter of the whole dinosaur story. Eoraptors eat all sorts of things, just like raccoons that munch on both fruits and small animals. It's like a dinosaur detective, always looking for clues that lead him to the next meal!

Seek & Find:

Reptile fossil   [1x]

Fern frond   [2x]

Amphibian   [1x]

Insect.   [1x]

Cycad leaf   [2x]

Raaaa-wr!!!
we don't just walk the forest; we own it.
#TrendsettingSinceTheTriassic"

In the next stop, Max visits the **Triassic Desert**, a landscape formed about 230 million years ago. This dry, sandy land has few green plants therefore is a big contrast to the lush forest. Max is amazed by the dinosaur that can live here, despite the hot weather and shortage of water.

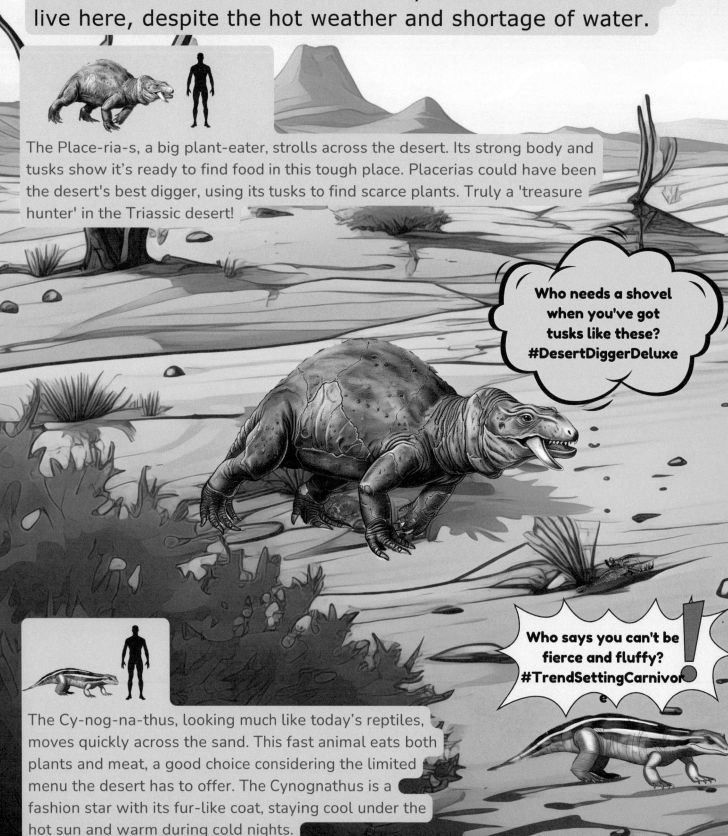

The Place-ria-s, a big plant-eater, strolls across the desert. Its strong body and tusks show it's ready to find food in this tough place. Placerias could have been the desert's best digger, using its tusks to find scarce plants. Truly a 'treasure hunter' in the Triassic desert!

Who needs a shovel when you've got tusks like these? #DesertDiggerDeluxe

Who says you can't be fierce and fluffy? #TrendSettingCarnivore

The Cy-nog-na-thus, looking much like today's reptiles, moves quickly across the sand. This fast animal eats both plants and meat, a good choice considering the limited menu the desert has to offer. The Cynognathus is a fashion star with its fur-like coat, staying cool under the hot sun and warm during cold nights.

The Po-sto-su-chus, a powerful predator, goes about the desert. Its large size and strong jaws give it a dominant presence in this rugged terrain. Postosuchus may have been the 'bully' of the Triassic Desert. As with its size and power, it surely has no problem grabbing the best sunbathing spots!

In the Triassic desert, size and smile matter. Guess I'm winning! #DesertDominator

Seek & Find:

Ancient insect [2x]

Petrified wood [2x]

Max arrives at the late **Triassic Riverbank**, a scene from 200 million years ago. This ancient riverbank buzzes with activities, as it's a place where green vegetation meets with winding rivers. The sounds of water and wildlife fill the air, creating a serene but exciting background for Max's new discovery.

The Coe-lo-phy-sis, known for its slim body and speed, wanders by the water. This swift dinosaur's long legs suggest it's a great runner. The Coelophysis could have been the champion sprinter of its time! Its light build and speed made it perfect for quick dashes along the riverbank, probably chasing insects or fish.

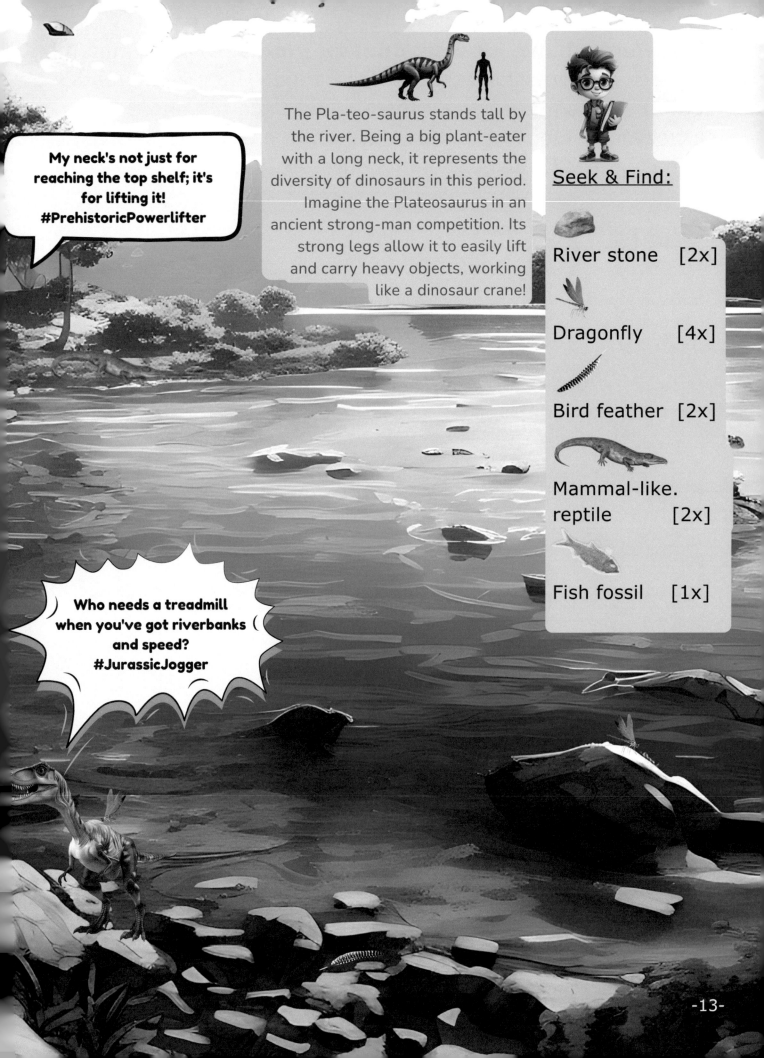

My neck's not just for reaching the top shelf; it's for lifting it! #PrehistoricPowerlifter

The Pla-teo-saurus stands tall by the river. Being a big plant-eater with a long neck, it represents the diversity of dinosaurs in this period. Imagine the Plateosaurus in an ancient strong-man competition. Its strong legs allow it to easily lift and carry heavy objects, working like a dinosaur crane!

Seek & Find:

River stone [2x]

Dragonfly [4x]

Bird feather [2x]

Mammal-like. reptile [2x]

Fish fossil [1x]

Who needs a treadmill when you've got riverbanks and speed? #JurassicJogger

Max returns to the **Jurassic Coastal Plains**, a fascinating mix of beach and grassland that existed about 165 million years ago! The green grassland stretches out from the shore like a carpet and the ocean sparkles like countless gems. This coast plain is indeed a bustling hub of Jurassic life.

The Allo-saurus is the Jurassic era's top hunter! With teeth like big scissors and claws as sharp as blades, this meat-eater is not to be taken lightly. And here's a thrilling possibility—scientists think the Allosaurus might have been the first to roar among dinosaurs! Imagine its powerful roar echoing along the coastline, sending chills to even the bravest dinosaurs!

With a bite this mighty, who needs to whisper? #JurassicJaws

The Di-lo-pho-saurus rushes along the shore like lightning. With its striking crest and speedy legs, this dinosaur is a pro at catching fish! Imagine the Dilophosaurus diving into the shallow waters and grabbing fish with its super fast reflexes. It's every Jurassic fisherman's dream!

The Ste-go-saurus has the most awesome back! It's covered in bumpy plates, like pieces of a giant puzzle. And you know what? Its tail also has spikes. Stegosaurus enjoys eating leaves all day. It could puff out its chest and stand tall, showing off its spiky back to both friends and enemies!

Eating greens and showing off my spikes—just a typical day in the Jurassic spa! #VeggieVogue

My crest isn't just for show—it's my secret to fishing success! #FashionForward Fisherman

Seek & Find:

Dinosaur footprint [1x]

Flower plant [2x]

Feather [1x]

Sea shell [2x]

Small lizard [2x]

Max steps into the **Jurassic Jungle**, a dense forest from the Late Jurassic era, over 160 million years ago. The jungle is filled with towering trees and thick bushes, creating a green canopy above with sunlight filtering through. And the distant roars of dinosaurs make the place quite mysterious.

The Bra-chio-saurus, a huge but gentle giant, stands tall above the jungle trees. Its head rises high as it quietly feeds on the tall tree leaves. The Brachiosaurus wouldn't be great playing hide and seek! Its massive size, up to 85 feet tall, would make it easily seen from anywhere.

Hide and seek? More like stand and peek! #GentleGiantPeekaboo

Who needs a runway when you've got the whole Jurassic sky? #FirstInFlight

The Ar-chae-opte-ryx, a bird-like dinosaur, flutters through the forest. Its feathers and wings suggest it might have been one of the first dinosaurs to fly. This ancient creature could have been the first daredevil flyer of the Jurassic era, hurray to the spirit of this airborne adventurer!

Seek & Find:

Amber stone [1x]

Dinosaur eggshell [1x]

Fern spore [3x]

Mammal fossil [1x]

Vine flower [4x]

Max comes across a big change from the lush jungle in the late **Jurassic Volcanic Landscape**, dating back 150 million years ago. The ground here is dotted with hot vents and streams of lava, creating a stunning yet daunting scene. Despite the sulfur smell and extreme heat, Max decides to continue with his exploration feeling both scared and excited.

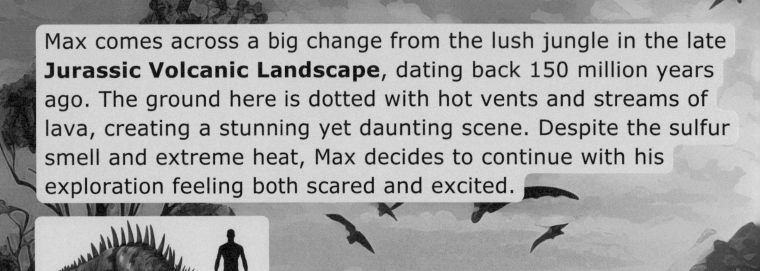

The Ken-tro-saurus, covered in cool spikes and plates, wanders around the vents. This little dinosaur is like a mini knight in spiky armor, showing how clever nature is at keeping creatures safe. Kentrosaurus is like a rock star of Jurassic world, wearing a 'spiky jacket' not just for good looks but also for staying safe from any trouble!

In the world of fashion and function, my spikes lead the charts! #PunkRockPaleo

Max arrives at the early **Cretaceous Floodplains**, a lively area from 120 million years ago. This place is full of wetlands and winding rivers, making it a perfect spot for plants to grow. With lots of different plants and plenty of water, it's a popular hang-out spot for many creatures of the Cretaceous period.

The I-gua-no-don, a tough plant-eater, walks across the floodplains. It's easy to spot with its unique thumb spikes and tough body, perfect for living in this green, watery environment. And guess what? Those thumb spikes aren't just for show; they're hidden tools for protection and finding food!

Thumbs up for survival! Who knew these spikes had so many uses? #ThumbSpikeLifeHack

Champion of hide-and-seek. Blink! and I'm gone! #StealthyStrider

The Psi-tta-co-saurus, a fast and small dinosaur, dashes around the floodplains. It has a very interesting look with a mouth like a bird's beak and can walk and run on two legs. The Psittacosaurus might have been a master at hide-and-seek in those days, it can quickly slip into the thick plants and disappear right under everyone's eyes.

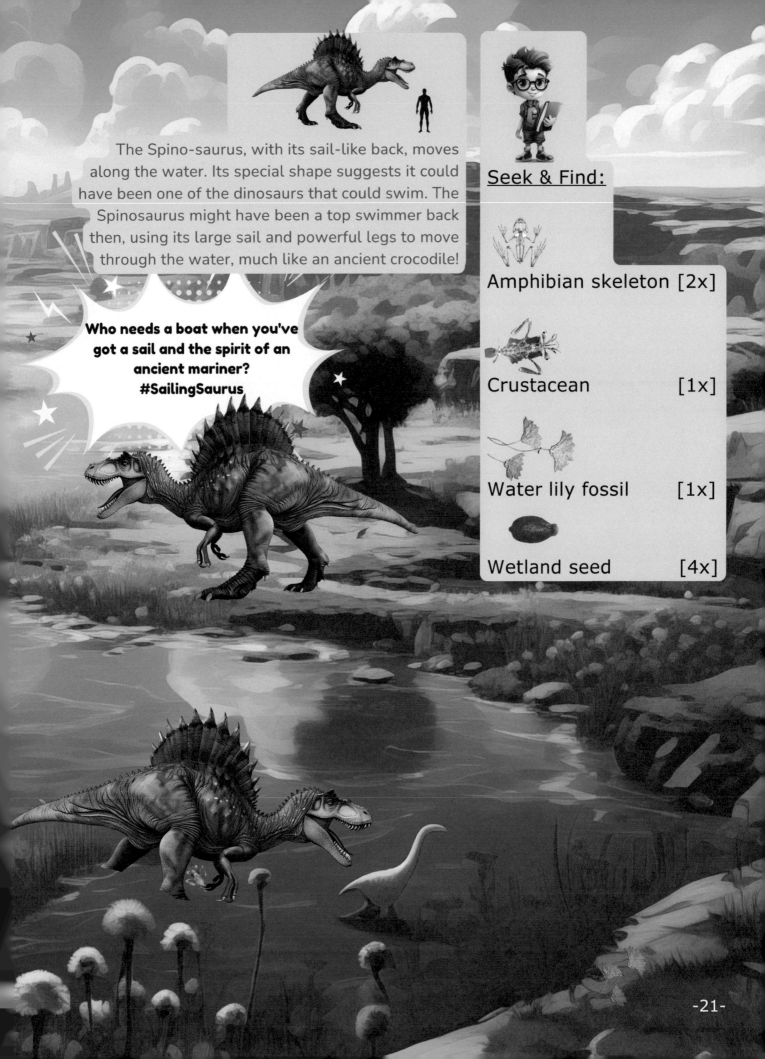

The Spino-saurus, with its sail-like back, moves along the water. Its special shape suggests it could have been one of the dinosaurs that could swim. The Spinosaurus might have been a top swimmer back then, using its large sail and powerful legs to move through the water, much like an ancient crocodile!

Who needs a boat when you've got a sail and the spirit of an ancient mariner?
#SailingSaurus

Seek & Find:

Amphibian skeleton [2x]

Crustacean [1x]

Water lily fossil [1x]

Wetland seed [4x]

Max enters the mid-**Cretaceous Forest** full of dense green plants and old tall trees, dating back 100 million years. The forest buzzes with the sounds and activities of so many different animals, showing what life is like a long, long time ago when it is most lively.

The An-ky-lo-saurus is a dinosaur with thick armor and a tail like a club. It moves slowly looking like a walking castle, as it uses armor for protection instead of speed. The Ankylosaurus could be compared to a tank - although it is not fast, it's not likely to be hurt and can break an enemy's bones with a swing of its tail!

Who needs speed when you're built like a fortress? #WalkingCastle

Push-ups? Please, I'd rather show off my roar-ups! #MightyHunter

The Ty-ran-no-saurus, the strongest predator, walks powerfully through the forest. Its large mouth and sturdy legs show how frightening predators can be. Tyrannosaurus's nickname is 'T-Rex' and have you ever imagined a T-Rex doing push-ups? Although it's the greatest hunter, its small arms aren't very useful for this exercise, as they only help T-Rex stay balanced.

Three horns, one mission: Keeping the Cretaceous safe and stylish! #TriHornChampion

The Tri-ce-ra-tops is a plant-eater with three large horns and a big neck shield. It moves through the bushes and is known for its strength and safety. The Triceratops was skilled at head-butting, using its horns like knights in a jousting match.

Seek & Find:

Bird nest. [1x]

Conifer cone [2x]

Flower fossil [2x]

Forest insect [4x]

Small rodent fossil [1x]

Max walks into the late **Cretaceous Swamps**, an area from 80 million years ago that has dark waters and green plants. The swamp is full of life, from tiny bugs to huge dinosaurs, all thriving in the damp and soggy environment.

The Ba-ry-o-nyx is a dinosaur that eats fish and lives near the swamp. It has long claws and a snout like a crocodile, which helps it catch fish in a unique way. The Baryonyx is probably the best fisherman of its time. It uses its special claws to scoop up fish from the water like a bear.

The Dei-no-su-chus, a giant ancient crocodile, hides in the swampy waters. Its huge size and strong jaws make it the top hunter in the swamp. The Deinosuchus might have been the very first 'water monster.' Being so big, it rules the swamp without any trouble!

Seek & Find:

Amphibian skeleton [2x]

Crocodile scale [2x]

Fish tooth [1x]

Swamp moss [4x]

Water plant [3x]

Scooping up dinner one claw at a time—swamp dining at its best! #SwampScooper

Who's the real swamp king? With jaws like these, there's no contest! #SwampSovereign

Max arrives at the late **Cretaceous Coastal Cliffs**, a breathtaking location from 75 million years ago. These tall cliffs stand over the ocean, offering a stunning view. It is a unique spot where the land and sea meet. The sound of the waves and the calls of ancient creatures fill the air, bringing the place to life.

The Pte-ra-no-don is a flying dinosaur that ruled the skies with its huge wings and fancy head crest. It is so good at flying that it can do lots of tricks in the air. Think of it like an old-time hang-glider, smoothly sailing on the sea winds.

The O-vi-raptor, a quick and lively dinosaur, dashes around the cliffs. With bird-like features and speedy moves, it makes this seaside area even more interesting. Even though "Oviraptor" means "egg thief," it might have been a good parent, protecting its nest strongly and never stealing. It could have been a hero of its time but misunderstood by many.

With moves like mine, who needs to steal? #AgileAvian

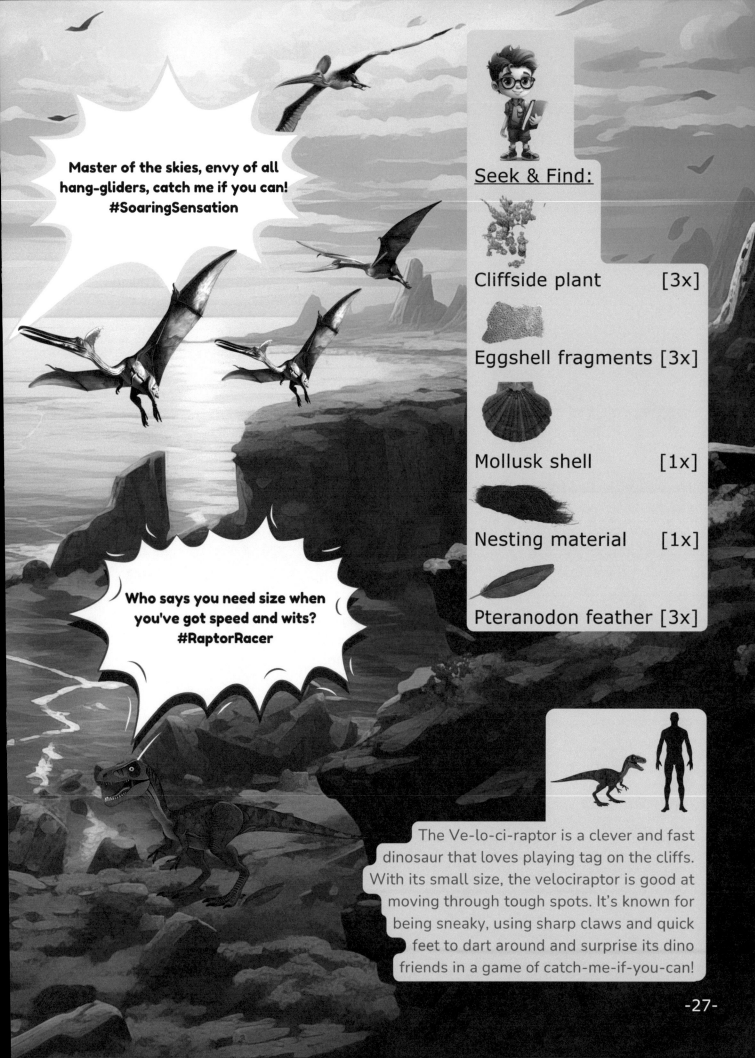

Master of the skies, envy of all hang-gliders, catch me if you can! #SoaringSensation

Seek & Find:

Cliffside plant [3x]

Eggshell fragments [3x]

Mollusk shell [1x]

Nesting material [1x]

Pteranodon feather [3x]

Who says you need size when you've got speed and wits? #RaptorRacer

The Ve-lo-ci-raptor is a clever and fast dinosaur that loves playing tag on the cliffs. With its small size, the velociraptor is good at moving through tough spots. It's known for being sneaky, using sharp claws and quick feet to dart around and surprise its dino friends in a game of catch-me-if-you-can!

Max is in the middle of an awesome dinosaur migration in the late **Cretaceous Plains** from 70 million years ago! He watches with wonder as large groups of dinosaurs walk across the open land on a huge adventure.

The Pro-to-ce-ra-tops, a little cousin of the Triceratops, hurries around the bigger dinosaurs. Its fancy frilled neck and beak-like mouth make it look quite special. The Protoceratops could have been the snack king of its time, using its beak to nibble on all sorts of tasty plants, making every meal a fun feast on the Great Plains!

The The-ri-zino-saurus, famous for its huge, hook-shaped claws, really catches the eye. Even though it looks pretty scary, it actually only eats plants. Its claws are super handy like a Swiss Army knife from nature! They could be used for finding food, staying safe, or showing off to other dinos.

From the plains to the forests, I'm the one with the rhythm and the reach! #CrestedVirtuoso

Who needs a big horn when you've got style and snacks? #SnackKing

The Pa-ra-sau-rolo-phus likes to walk with its group. No matter where it goes it is easy to spot due to the way it stands on two legs and its colorful crest that leans back. The Parasaurolophus may have been the first 'jazz musician', as it's able to create deep, echoing sounds with its hollow crest like a natural trombone.

The Co-ry-tho-saurus, sporting a cool helmet-looking crest, strolls around the plains. This dino with a duck bill is famous for its fancy headgear and the habit of hanging out in groups. The crest on the Corythosaurus isn't just for looks; it can work like a built-in trumpet, letting Corythosaurus make noises or even play fun tunes to its dino buddies!

Seek & Find:

Dinosaur egg fossil [1x]

Flying
Dinosaur feather [4x]

Dinosaur footprint [4x]

Fossilized leaf [3x]

Prehistoric seed [2x]

Looking sharp, eating greens, living the peaceful dino dream. #ClawsForThought

Gather round, dino pals, and let's turn these plains into a concert! #CretaceousMusician

Max finds himself at a huge turning point in Earth's story coming to the **Cretaceous-Paleogene (K-Pg) Boundary**, 66 million years back. These places are dark and fiery, showing Max the big events changing the planet forever. Bit by bit, Max now gets the secrets of why the dinosaur era came to an end.

This time marks a huge change, with signs of a big asteroid hitting earth and lots of volcanoes erupting. The places that used to be full of all kinds of dinosaurs are changing, making way for mammals and birds to become the main characters in the story of our planet.

Imagine this turning point where dinosaurs disappear all of a sudden, leaving behind a hidden collection of fossils to explore. The K-Pg Boundary shows how exciting discoveries can be made, and how vulnerable the entire dinosaur family could be. It's a lesson about the strength of nature and how life's story is always changing.

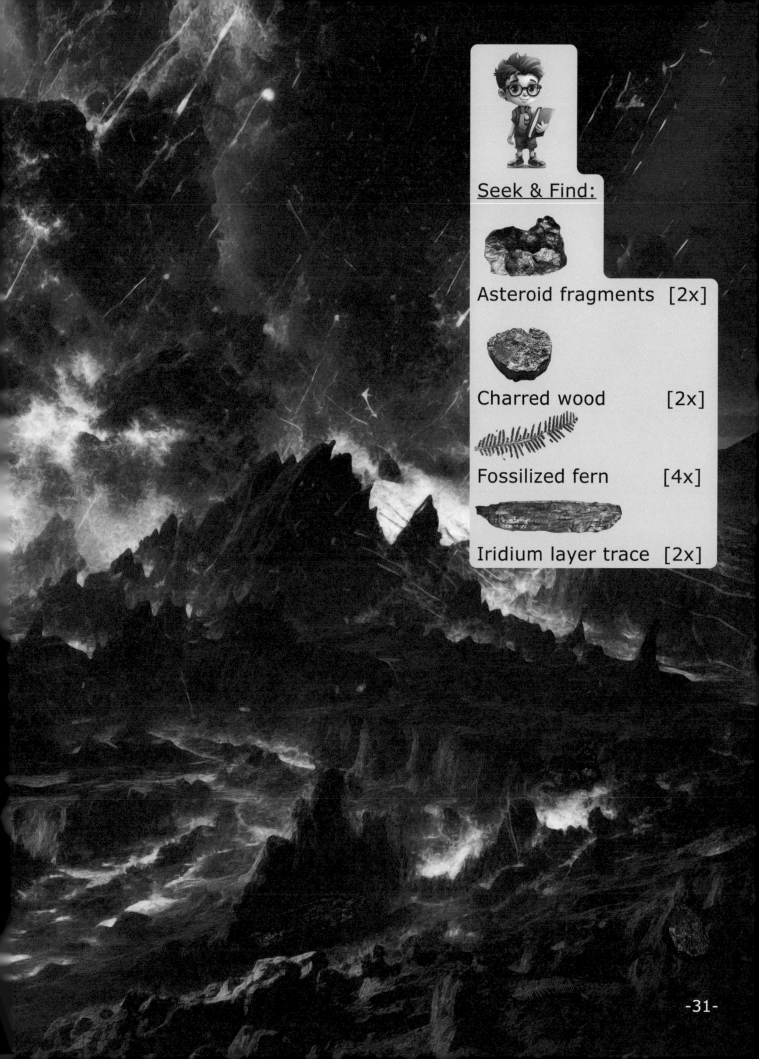

Now with all the items gathered from the map, Max begins to feel dizzy as things get blurred in front of his eyes. He knows it's because Dr. Dino is pulling him back to the present day to reveal the secrets. Heartbroken to see the remarkable dinosaurs vanish into those horrible natural events, Max slowly finds himself putting hands back on the attic door.

Professor! What an adventure!

Great job Max! I'm sure you've seen pieces of the secrets with your own eyes! And for your friends who don't know yet, I've just put all the findings into this secret-revealing book.

Then Professor Dino starts time traveling to the future to inspire the kids there about dinosaurs too! Before disappearing he says: Go share the secret book with your friends Max, and maybe we'll meet again sometime!...

Clue Page

Triassic Forest

Triassic Desert

Triassic Riverbank

Jurassic Coastal Plains

Jurassic Jungle

Jurassic Volcanic Landscape

Clue Page

Cretaceous Floodplains

Cretaceous Forest

Cretaceous Swamps

Cretaceous Coastal Cliffs

Cretaceous Plains

K-Pg Boundary

Glossary

Amber - tree sap that turned into a golden treasure, sometimes with tiny fossils inside

Amphibian - animals like a frog that can live in both water and on land

Crustacean - sea bugs with hard shells, and they live in the ocean or lakes

Cycad - super old plants that look like a mix between a palm tree and a fern

Fossil - a very old clue about an animal or plant from long ago

Gastrolith - rocks in dinosaur tummy, they help grind up touch food

K-Pg Boundary - A line in history marking the big crash that ended dinosaurs' reign

Mammal - warm-blooded, furry animals who drink milk as babies

Mollusk - animals with soft bodies, live in shells for protection

Moss - a tiny, green carpet that grows in damp places, like on trees

Reptile - animals that lay eggs and have scales instead of fur

Rodent - small animals with big front teeth, like squirrels, mice, hamsters

Acknowledgements:

A Journey Shared:

To the stars of this adventure who illuminated the path not just for Max, but for me—thank you.

My heartfelt gratitude to my beloved wife, Joling, for unwavering support; and my 8-year -old son, Alex, for enriching my imagination; also to my designer Ale and whole team, for offering laughter and insights that shaped this tale...

This book is a tapestry of your support and love, woven into every page.

About the Author

Jamie Whimsy: Storyteller, Traveller, Dinosaur Enthusiast:

Jamie writes tales that blend fantasy with reality, exploring human experiences through imaginative stories.

With a passion for traveling, Jamie also draws inspirations from trips to deep nature, he especially likes the expeditions in the land of Africa. Jamie believes in the magic of storytelling to inspire, teach, and connect us all, one dinosaur footprint at a time.

More interactive contents based on this book can be found at Jamie Whimsy's social channels:

Instagram

Youtube

Made in United States
Troutdale, OR
11/10/2024